The Cornbread Cookbook

Cornbread, Cakes and Muffins

for Every Occasion

Table of Contents

Introduction 4

   1. Homesteader cornbread 6

   2. Healthy cornbread 8

   3. Sweet buttermilk cornbread 10

   5. Jalapeno and beer cornbread 13

   6. Honey Cornbread 16

   7. Mexican cornbread 18

   8. Sweet jalapeno cornbread 21

   9. Quick and Easy cornbread 23

   10. Golden Sweet cornbread 25

   11. Basic corn muffins 27

   12. Corndog muffins 29

   13. Sweet corn cake 31

   14. Sweet cornbread cake 34

   15. Sweet cornbread 36

   16. Amusement park cornbread 38

   17. Camp cornbread 40

   18. Best ever corn muffins 42

   19. Berry cornmeal muffins 44

   20. Sweet jalapeno cornbread II 46

   21. Most wonderful cornbread 48

   22. Southwestern corn pup muffins 50

23. Pumpkin cornbread 53

24. Broccoli cheese cornbread 55

25. Blue cornbread 57

26. Molasses cornbread 59

27. Onion cheese cornbread 61

28. Coconut oil cornbread 63

29. Honey cornbread muffins 65

30. Pumpkin polenta cornbread 67

Conclusion 69

Introduction

Are you looking for delicious cornbread recipes that are simple to make and inexpensive to shop for? Do you want a side dish to serve with your meals that is healthy and filling? Then look no further than the cornbread cookbook filled with tasty recipes. For thousand of years natives of North America have been using corn meal in recipes long before settlers came to this country. The delicious flavour and plentiful supply of corn ensured food to feed villages of families and the consistency was thicker than flour and kept the stomach full for longer. Cornmeal is normally fried or baked to produce treats such as cornbread, corn muffins or cornbread cake that completes a meal when served with soups, stews and chilis. The sweeter cornbread is for cake at parties and gatherings and is often served with other sweet treats like fruit or yogurt.

1.Homesteader cornbread

I like to eat this delicious cornbread with some chili or soup. You can also enjoy this recipe as a side dish for almost any meal.

Preparation Time-15 minutes

Servings - 15

Ingredients

- 12 ounces cornmeal *1½ C*
- 20 ounces milk *2¾ C*
- 16 ounces all-purpose flour *3 ⅔ C*
- 1/2 ounce baking powder *1 TBS*
- 1 teaspoon salt
- 5 1/2 ounces white sugar *⅔ C*
- 2 large eggs
- 4 ounces vegetable oil

Directions

Preheat oven to 400 degrees Fahrenheit. Coat a 9x13 baking pan with cooking spray.

Mix cornmeal and milk in a bowl and let sit for 5 minutes.

In a separate bowl, whisk flour, baking powder, sugar and salt until well combined.

Stir cornmeal mixture into flour mixture. Mix in eggs and oil and stir until smooth.

Pour batter into baking pan and bake for 30-35 minutes until a tester comes out clean.

2. Healthy cornbread

When you want a healthier option for cornbread, try this simple recipe. I like to have this with a salad and soup for lunch.

Preparation Time - 10 minutes

Servings - 12

Ingredients

- 8 ounces unbleached flour
- 8 ounces cornmeal
- 2 ounces white sugar

- 1 teaspoon baking soda
- 3/4 teaspoon salt
- 8 ounces plain nonfat yogurt
- 2 beaten eggs

Directions

Preheat oven to 400 degrees Fahrenheit. Coat an 8"x8" baking pan with cooking spray.

Whisk flour, sugar, baking soda, cornmeal and salt in a large bowl until well combined.

Stir yogurt and eggs into the dry mixture until just moistened.

Pour batter into baking pan and bake for 20-25 minutes until the tester comes out clean.

3. Sweet buttermilk cornbread

This cornbread is sweet enough to have for dessert or a special treat for breakfast with coffee. The flavour is delightful and everyone will love it.

Preparation Time-10 minutes

Servings - 10

Ingredients

- 2 ounces vegetable oil
- 16 ounces white cornmeal
- 6 ounces all-purpose flour
- 2 1/2 ounces white sugar
- 3/4 ounce baking powder
- 1 teaspoon salt
- 1/2 teaspoon baking soda
- 2 large eggs
- 16 ounces buttermilk

Directions

Preheat oven to 450 degrees Fahrenheit.

Pour oil into a 10" oven-safe frying pan and swirl around to coat the bottom and sides.

Put pan in the oven for 3-5 minutes and remove when oil is very hot.

In a large bowl, whisk together flour, cornmeal, baking soda, baking powder and salt.

In another large bowl, beat eggs until light and fluffy. Stir in buttermilk until well combined.

Pour 1 ounce of oil from the hot pan into the egg mixture and beat until fully incorporated.

Stir egg mixture into the dry flour mixture until moistened and smooth. Pour batter into frying pan and bake for 18-20 minutes until a tester comes out clean.

5. Jalapeno and beer cornbread

Try this cornbread with a cold glass of ale and some hot chili. The spicy flavour of the jalapeno in this bread is addictive.

You can use any bread of dark ale for this recipe, I just prefer Pilsner.

Preparation Time-15 minutes

Servings - 8

Ingredients

- 8 ounces cornmeal
- 1 teaspoon baking powder
- 4 ounces buttermilk
- 4 ounces Pilsner beer
- 1 teaspoon salt
- 4 ounces melted butter
- 8 ounces all-purpose flour
- 2 beaten eggs
- 2 1/2 ounces white sugar
- 4 chopped green onions
- 1 teaspoon baking soda
- 1 chopped jalapeno pepper

Directions

Preheat oven to 400 degrees Fahrenheit. Coat a baking pan with cooking spray.

In a large bowl, whisk together the cornmeal, baking powder, flour, salt and baking soda until combined.

In another bowl, combine buttermilk, butter and beer. Stir in dry flour mixture to the wet mixture gradually until moistened.

Stir egg and sugar into the batter and fold in onions and jalapeno.

Pour batter into the baking pan and bake for 30-35 minutes until a tester comes out clean.

6.Honey Cornbread

The sweet flavour of cornbread is mouthwatering and delicious. Try serving this as a sweet snack with some hot tea and fresh fruit.

Preparation Time-10 minutes

Servings - 8

- 8 ounces all-purpose flour
- 8 ounces yellow cornmeal

- 2 ounces white sugar
- 1/2 ounce baking powder
- 8 ounces heavy cream
- 2 ounces vegetable oil
- 2 ounces honey
- 2 lightly beaten eggs

Directions

Preheat the oven to 400 degrees Fahrenheit. Coat a 9" baking pan with cooking spray.

Whisk the cornmeal, flour, baking powder and sugar in a large bowl and make a well in the middle of the mixture.

In a separate bowl, stir cream, oil, honey and eggs together. Pour wet mixture into the well in the middle of the flour mixture and stir until just combined.

Pour batter into baking pan and bake for 20-25 minutes until a tester comes out clean.

7.Mexican cornbread

The spicy cornbread is perfect for chili dinners or with some hot beans. Use the cornbread to mop up any excess sauce.

Preparation Time-10 minutes

Servings - 6

Ingredients

- 8 ounces melted butter
- 8 ounces white sugar
- 4 large eggs
- 15 ounces canned creamed corn

- 2 ounces drained canned green chile peppers, chopped
- 4 ounces Monterey Jack cheese, shredded
- 4 ounces Cheddar cheese, shredded
- 8 ounces all-purpose flour
- 8 ounces yellow cornmeal
- 2/3 ounce baking powder
- 1/4 teaspoon salt

Directions

Preheat oven to 300 degrees Fahrenheit. Coat a 13x9 baking dish with cooking spray.

Cream butter and sugar together in a large bowl with an electric mixer.

Beat eggs into the mixture one at a time, incorporating fully before the next addition.

Blend in corn, green chiles, Monterey Jack and cheddar cheeses.

Sift all-purpose flour, cornmeal, salt and baking powder together in a large bowl.

Stir dry flour mixture into the wet mixture until smooth and combined.

Pour batter into baking dish and bake for 60 minutes until a tester comes out clean.

8. Sweet jalapeno cornbread

The combination of sweet and spicy makes this cornbread recipe one my favourites. Try this with some hot soup or stew for dinner.

Preparation Time-15 minutes

Servings - 8

Ingredients

- 5 1/2 ounces softened margarine
- 5 1/2 ounces white sugar
- 16 ounces cornmeal
- 10 1/2 ounces all-purpose flour

- 3/4 ounce baking powder
- 3 large eggs
- 1 teaspoon salt
- 13 1/2 ounces milk
- 8 ounces fresh jalapeno peppers, chopped

Directions

Preheat oven to 400 degrees Fahrenheit. Coat a 13x9 baking dish with cooking spray.

In a large mixing bowl, cream margarine and sugar together until smooth.

In a separate bowl, whisk cornmeal, flour, salt and baking powder together until well combined.

In a 3rd large bowl, beat eggs and milk together until combined.

Alternating between milk and flour mixture, stir 1/3 of each mixture into the bowl with margarine until batter is just combined. Repeat process until all the batter is combined.

Fold peppers into the batter and pour into the baking pan.

Bake for 22-26 minutes until a tester comes out clean.

9. Quick and Easy cornbread

Give this recipe a try when you want a delicious side dish quickly. The moist texture of this cornbread will melt in your mouth with each bite.

Preparation Time-15 minutes

Servings - 8

Ingredients

- 24 ounces all-purpose flour
- 24 ounces cornmeal
- 8 ounces white sugar
- 1 1/2 ounces baking powder
- 1 teaspoon salt

- 24 ounces whole milk
- 8 ounces vegetable oil
- 3 large eggs

Directions

1. Preheat oven to 400 degrees Fahrenheit. Coat a 10x15 baking pan with cooking spray.

2. In a large bowl, whisk together cornmeal, baking powder, flour, sugar and salt until well combined. Stir the rest of the **Ingredients** into the flour mixture until combined and moistened.

3. Pour batter into baking pan and bake for 33 minutes until a tester comes out clean.

10. Golden Sweet cornbread

The sweet flavour of this cornbread tastes amazing with some hot coffee and fresh berries. I like to have this for breakfast on the weekends for a treat.

Preparation Time-10 minutes

Servings - 12

Ingredients

- 8 ounces all-purpose flour
- 8 ounces yellow cornmeal
- 5 1/2 ounces white sugar
- 1 teaspoon salt
- 3 1/2 teaspoons baking powder
- 1 large egg
- 8 ounces milk
- 2 1/2 ounces vegetable oil

Directions

Preheat oven to 400 degrees Fahrenheit. Coat a 9" round baking pan with cooking spray.

Whisk flour, cornmeal, salt, sugar and baking powder in a large bowl until well combined. Add egg, oil and milk to the flour mixture until fully incorporated.

Pour batter into the baking pan and bake for 20-25 minutes until a tester comes out clean.

11.Basic corn muffins

These individually-sized muffins make the perfect snack to pack and go. I like to bring a few of these to work with me for the afternoon munchies.

Preparation Time-10 minutes

Servings - 12

Ingredients

- 8 ounces cornmeal
- 8 ounces all-purpose flour
- 2 1/2 ounces white sugar
- 1/3 ounce baking powder
- 1/2 teaspoon salt
- 1 beaten egg
- 2 ounces canola oil
- 8 ounces milk

Directions

Preheat oven to 400 degrees Fahrenheit. Line a 12-cup muffin tin with the paper liners.

Whisk flour, cornmeal, sugar, baking powder and salt in a large bowl until well combined.

Stir in oil, egg and milk until combined.

Evenly distribute batter between the muffin cups and bake for 15-20 minutes until a tester comes out clean.

12. Corndog muffins

The kids will go crazy for these savoury muffins when they find them in their lunch. I like to eat these with some mustard or garlic dipping sauce.

Preparation Time-10 minutes

Servings - 12

Ingredients

- 8 1/2 ounces cornbread mix
- 1 ounce brown sugar
- 2 large eggs

- 12 ounces milk
- 8 ounces Cheddar cheese, grated
- 9 halved hot dogs

Directions

Preheat oven to 400 degrees Fahrenheit. Line a 12-cup muffin tin with the paper liners.

In a large mixing bowl, combine brown sugar and cornbread mix.

In a separate bowl, beat eggs and milk together until smooth.

Stir eggs into the brown sugar mixture with the cheese until just combined.

Evenly divide batter between the muffin cups and then bake for 14-18 minutes until a tester comes out clean.

13.Sweet corn cake

This sweet cake is always a hit at gatherings, especially in the summer. I like to serve this when I have some beef stew or spicy chili.

Preparation Time-15 minutes

Servings - 6

Ingredients

- 4 ounces softened butter
- 2 1/2 ounces masa harina
- 2 ounces water

- 12 ounces thawed frozen whole-kernel corn
- 2 ounces cornmeal
- 2 1/2 ounces white sugar
- 1 ounce heavy whipping cream
- 1/2 teaspoon baking powder
- 1/4 teaspoon salt

Directions

Preheat oven to 350 degrees Fahrenheit.

Cream butter with an electric mixer in a medium bowl. Add corn flour and water and beat the mixture until well combined.

Place thawed corn in a blender and pulse until mildly chunky, Stir butter into the corn.

In another mixing bowl, whisk together cornmeal, sugar, salt, cream and baking powder.

Stir cornflour mixture into cornmeal mixture until combined.

Transfer batter to an 8" baking pan and cover with foil.

Fill a 13x9 baking dish with water 2/3 up and place 8" baking pan inside.

Bake for 50-60 minutes. Remove from oven and cool for 10 minutes.

14.Sweet cornbread cake

This recipe is another for sweet cornbread cake that the family will love. I like to serve this with some yogurt and fresh berries.

Preparation Time-15 minutes

Servings - 12

Ingredients

- 8 ounces cornmeal
- 24 ounces all-purpose flour

- 10 1/2 ounces white sugar
- 1 ounce baking powder
- 1 teaspoon salt
- 5 1/2 ounces vegetable oil
- 2 1/2 ounces butter, melted
- 1 ounce honey
- 4 beaten eggs
- 20 ounces whole milk

Directions

Preheat the oven to 350 degrees Fahrenheit. Coat a 9x13 baking pan with cooking spray.

In a large bowl, whisk sugar, cornmeal, baking powder, flour and salt together until well combined.

In a separate bowl, mix oil, butter, honey, eggs and milk. Stir the wet mixture into the dry mixture until just moistened.

Pour batter into the prepared baking pan and bake for 45 minutes until top begins to brown and crack slightly.

15. Sweet cornbread

I love sweet cornbread for dinner when I am serving a glazed ham or chili. Try a slice when you are feeling hungry in between meals for a tasty snack.

Preparation Time-15 minutes

Servings - 9

Ingredients

- 8 ounces all-purpose flour
- 8 ounces cornmeal
- 2 ounces white sugar

- 1/2 teaspoon baking soda
- 1/2 teaspoon salt
- 1 lightly beaten egg
- 1/2 teaspoon of baking powder
- 8 ounces sour cream
- 2 1/2 ounces milk
- 2 ounces melted butter

Directions

Preheat oven to 400 degrees Fahrenheit. Coat an 8x8 baking pan with cooking spray.

In a large bowl, whisk sugar, flour, baking soda, cornmeal, baking powder and salt until well combined.

In a separate bowl, beat egg, milk, sour cream and butter together.

Fold wet mixture into dry mixture until just combined and transfer to baking pan.

Bake for 20-25 minutes until a tester comes out clean.

16.Amusement park cornbread

My childhood memories consist of going to the fair and buying a delicious slice of special cornbread. This recipe comes closest to the flavour I remember.

Preparation Time-15 minutes

Servings - 8

Ingredients

- 5 1/2 ounces white sugar

- 1 teaspoon salt
- 2 1/2 ounces softened butter, softened
- 1 teaspoon vanilla extract
- 2 large eggs
- 16 ounces all-purpose flour
- 1/2 ounce baking powder
- 6 ounces cornmeal
- 10 1/2 ounces milk

Directions

Preheat oven to 400 degrees Fahrenheit. Coat an 8" oven-safe frying pan with cooking spray.

Beat sugar, butter, salt and vanilla together in a large mixing bowl until smooth and creamy. Add eggs to the sugar mixture one at a time, beating well in between

Whisk flour, baking powder and cornmeal together in a large bowl. Alternate stirring milk and flour mixture into the egg until well combined.

Pour batter into frying pan and place in the oven for 20 minutes until a tester comes out clean.

17. Camp cornbread

If you ever went to sleepover camp, you will probably remember the cornbread served with the evening meal. I found this recipe evokes those happy memories.

Preparation Time-5 minutes

Servings - 8

Ingredients

- 8 oz pkg corn bread muffin mix
- 2 1/2 ounces milk

- 1 lightly beaten egg
- 8 ounces canned cream corn
- 4 ounces white sugar

Directions

Preheat the oven to 350 degrees Fahrenheit. Coat a 9x13 baking pan with a cooking spray.

Stir milk and egg into a large bowl with muffin mix. Mix in corn and sugar until combined and pour the batter into baking pan.

Then bake for about 30 minutes until a toothpick inserted in the middle comes out clean.

18. Best ever corn muffins

These muffins make a great snack or breakfast. I like to have one hot out of the oven with some butter.

Preparation Time-15 minutes

Servings - 12

Ingredients

- 2 ounces softened butter
- 4 1/2 ounces white sugar
- 2 large eggs
- 1/2 ounce vanilla extract

- 12 ounces biscuit baking mix
- 2 ounces yellow cornmeal
- 5 1/2 ounces milk

Directions

Preheat oven to 375 degrees Fahrenheit. Line a 12-cup muffin tin with the paper liners.

Cream the butter and sugar together using an electric mixer until fluffy. Add the eggs one at a time, and beat well before each addition. Stir in vanilla.

Whisk baking mix and cornmeal in another bowl. Stir dry cornmeal mix into the wet butter mix until just combined and evenly divide batter between the muffin cups.

Then bake for 20-30 minutes until golden brown and a tester comes out clean.

19. Berry cornmeal muffins

These strawberry cornbread muffins make a sweet treat in the morning with a hot tea. I have used frozen strawberries but fresh is best.

Preparation Time - 15 minutes

Servings - 12

Ingredients

- 8 ounces all-purpose flour
- 6 ounces cornmeal

- 4 ounces white sugar
- 1/2 ounce baking powder
- 1/4 teaspoon salt
- 16 ounces fresh strawberries, chopped
- 8 ounces naturally-flavored strawberry yogurt
- 2 ounces melted butter
- 1 lightly beaten egg

Directions

Preheat oven to 350 degrees Fahrenheit. Line a 12-cup muffin tin with paper liners.

Then whisk cornmeal, baking powder, flour, sugar and salt in a large bowl.

Gently toss strawberries with 4 ounces of flour in another bowl.

Beat egg, butter and yogurt and stir into the flour mixture until just combined. Fold strawberries into the batter and evenly divide between muffin liners.

Bake for 25 minutes until a tester comes out clean.

20. Sweet jalapeno cornbread II

This recipe uses a natural sugar substitute for dietary restrictions. The Stevia has a unique taste that makes the cornbread extra sweet without an aftertaste.

Preparation Time-15 minutes

Servings - 12

Ingredients

- 5 1/2 ounces softened margarine
- 5 1/2 ounces Stevia

- 16 ounces cornmeal
- 10 1/2 ounces all-purpose flour
- 1 teaspoon salt 3/4 ounce baking powder
- 3 eggs
- 13 1/2 ounces buttermilk
- 8 ounces fresh jalapeno peppers, chopped

Directions

Preheat oven to 400 degrees Fahrenheit. Coat a 9x13 baking dish with a cooking spray.

Cream margarine and Stevia together with an electric mixer in a large bowl until smooth.

In another bowl, mix cornmeal, baking powder, flour and salt until well combined.

In a third bowl, beat eggs and buttermilk together. Combine 1/3 of each mixture together in the bowl with the margarine until just combined. Repeat process twice more.

Stir in jalapenos and pour batter into baking pan.

Bake for 22-26 minutes until a tester comes out clean.

21. Most wonderful cornbread

The title says it all in this wonderful cornbread. Serve this recipe as a side dish for dinner when serving meat and salad.

Preparation Time-10 minutes

Servings - 12

Ingredients

- 8 oz package dry cornbread mix
- 2 large eggs
- 4 ounces chopped broccoli, cooked

- 4 ounces onion, chopped
- 4 ounces cottage cheese
- 2 1/2 ounces melted butter

Directions

Preheat oven to 350 degrees Fahrenheit. Coat an 8" square pan with cooking spray.

Mix all the **Ingredients** together until well combined and pour into baking pan.

Bake for 40 minutes until a tester put in the center comes out clean.

22. Southwestern corn pup muffins

The Monterey Jack cheese gives these muffins a delicious Southwestern kick that tastes amazing with some dipping sauce. The moist muffins melt in your mouth and you will be reaching for seconds while chewing the first.

Preparation Time-15 minutes

Servings - 12

Ingredients

- 6 ounces yellow cornmeal
- 8 ounces all-purpose flour
- 2 1/2 ounces white sugar
- 1/2 ounce baking powder
- 1/2 teaspoon salt
- 1 teaspoon ground cumin
- 1 teaspoon chili powder
- 1 teaspoon garlic powder
- 8 ounces milk
- 1 beaten egg
- 1 ounce canola oil
- 2 1/2 ounces Monterey Jack cheese, shredded
- 4 hot dogs, sliced in 1" pieces

Dipping Sauce:

- 4 ounces sour cream
- 4 ounces mayonnaise
- 3/4 ounce dry taco seasoning mix

Directions

Preheat the oven to 400 degrees Fahrenheit. Line two 12-cup muffin tins with paper liners.

Whisk cornmeal, sugar, flour, salt, baking powder, salt, chili, garlic and cumin together in a large bowl until well combined.

Make a well in the middle of the dry **Ingredients** and pour in egg, milk and oil. Stir mixture until combined and gradually stir cheese into the batter.

Spoon a small amount of batter into each muffin liner and add a hot dog piece to the batter. Fill the rest of the liner with batter to cover the hot dog and bake for 10-12 minutes until a tester comes out clean.

While muffins are cooking, whisk the dipping sauce **Ingredients** together until well combined and serve with the muffins.

23.Pumpkin cornbread

Gourds are used in many delicious recipes in the Fall when the ingredient is plentiful. I like to serve this with some whipped cream or fresh fruit.

Preparation Time-15 minutes

Servings - 12

Ingredients

- 8 ounces all-purpose flour

- 6 ounces yellow cornmeal
- 1/2 teaspoon baking soda 1 teaspoon baking powder
- 1/4 teaspoon salt
- 2 well-beaten eggs,
- 8 ounces canned pumpkin puree, unsweetened
- 4 ounces dark brown sugar, packed
- 2 ounces canola oil
- 8 ounces pecans, coarsely chopped

Directions

Preheat the oven to 425 degrees Fahrenheit. Line a 12-cup muffin tin with paper liners.

Whisk the flour, baking soda, cornmeal, baking powder and salt in a large bowl until well combined.

Stir pumpkin puree, eggs, sugar and oil in another bowl.

Make a well in the middle of the flour mixture and pour the wet mixture into the well. Stir until just moistened.

Fold nuts into the batter and divide evenly between the muffin cups.

Bake for 15-18 minutes until a tester comes out clean.

24. Broccoli cheese cornbread

This cornbread is a lovely side dish for dinner or lunch. I have also cut it into small pieces and served it as an appetizer with some dipping sauce.

Preparation Time-15 minutes

Servings - 12

- 4 large eggs
- 10 ounce pkg. thawed frozen broccoli, drained and chopped

- 8 ounces cottage cheese
- 1 chopped onion
- 4 ounces melted butter
- 8 1/2 ounces self-rising cornmeal
- 1 teaspoon salt

Directions

Preheat oven to 400 degrees Fahrenheit. Coat a 7x11 baking pan with cooking spray.

Mix cornmeal and salt in a large bowl.

In another bowl, stir eggs, onion, cottage cheese and butter together until combined.

Stir wet mixture into the cornmeal mixture until just moistened. Fold broccoli into the batter and pour into the baking pan.

Bake for 30 minutes until a tester inserted in the middle comes out clean.

25. Blue cornbread

The blue cornmeal gives this recipe a unique appearance and a delicious taste. I like to make this cornbread for dinner when I want to make a special meal.

Preparation Time-15 minutes

Servings - 16

- 8 ounces blue cornmeal
- 8 ounces all-purpose flour
- 5 teaspoons baking powder
- 2 ounces white sugar

- a pinch salt
- 2 beaten eggs
- 8 ounces milk
- 4 ounces butter

Directions

Preheat an oven to 350 degrees Fahrenheit. Coat a 9" baking dish with cooking spray.

Sift flour, cornmeal, baking powder, sugar and salt together in a large bowl. Do this 2-3 times more to fully combine.

Stir milk and eggs into the flour mixture until just moistened.

Melt butter in the baking dish by placing it in the oven. Stir melted butter into the batter and pour into the baking dish.

Bake for 30-35 minutes until a tester inserted in the middle comes out clean.

26.Molasses cornbread

The molasses gives this cornbread a moist texture you will love. Try this with some chili or stew for your next meal.

Preparation Time-15 minutes

Servings - 12

Ingredients

- 5 1/2 ounces cornmeal
- 6 ounces all-purpose flour
- 1/2 ounce baking powder
- 1 teaspoon salt
- 1 beaten egg

- 8 ounces milk
- 1 ounce molasses

Directions

Preheat the oven to 400 degrees Fahrenheit. Coat an 8" baking pan with cooking spray.

Whisk flour, cornmeal, salt and baking powder in a large bowl until well combined.

Beat egg, molasses and milk together in a separate bowl. Stir wet mixture into dry mixture until moistened and pour into baking pan.

Bake for 15-20 minutes until a tester inserted in the middle comes out clean.

27.Onion cheese cornbread

The onion and sour cream add an amazing flavour to this cornbread you will find addictive. I serve this as a side dish when I cook lamb or steak.

Preparation Time-15 minutes

Servings - 12

Ingredients

- 1 large chopped onion
- 16 ounces sour cream
- 2 beaten eggs

- 15 1/4 ounces canned cream-style white corn
- 1/2 teaspoon ground white pepper
- 4 ounces butter, unsalted
- 16 ounces white cornbread mix
- 5 1/2 ounces buttermilk
- 1/2 teaspoon salt
- 16 ounces sharp Cheddar cheese, shredded

Directions

Preheat the oven to 400 degrees Fahrenheit. Coat a 13x9 baking dish with cooking spray.

Melt butter in a frying pan on medium heat and sauté onions in the butter until translucent. Remove onions from heat and stir in sour cream.

Combine cornbread mix, beaten eggs, corn, buttermilk, salt and pepper in a large bowl until smooth. Pour batter into the baking dish and smooth down to make it even.

Add 1/2 of the cheddar cheese to the onions and sour cream and spread over the batter in the pan.

Top with the remaining cheese and bake for 25-30 minutes until a tester inserted in the center comes out clean.

28.Coconut oil cornbread

The coconut oil has a refreshing flavour that tastes amazing in this recipe. I like to serve this with some fresh butter.

Preparation Time-15 minutes

Servings - 15

Ingredients

- 20 ounces milk
- 12 ounces cornmeal

- 16 ounces all-purpose flour
- 4 ounces white sugar
- 4 ounces melted coconut oil
- 3/4 ounce baking powder
- 1 teaspoon salt
- 2 beaten eggs

Directions

Preheat the oven to 400 degrees Fahrenheit. Coat a 13x9 baking dish with cooking spray.

In a bowl, combine cornmeal and milk until moistened and soak for 5-6 minutes.

Whisk sugar, flour, baking powder and salt together in another bowl. Stir in cornmeal mixture, eggs and oil. Mix until smooth.

Then pour the batter into baking dish and bake for 30-35 minutes until a tester comes out clean.

29.Honey cornbread muffins

These muffins make an amazing breakfast with some fresh fruit and yogurt. The honey adds a lovely natural sweetness you will love.

Preparation Time-15 minutes

Servings - 12

Ingredients

- 8 ounces enriched yellow corn meal
- 8 ounces All Purpose Flour
- 1/2 ounce baking powder

- 1/2 teaspoon ground cinnamon
- 1 lightly beaten egg
- 4 ounces milk
- 4 ounces honey
- 2 1/2 ounces Corn Oil
- 2 ounces sour cream

Directions

Heat oven to 400 degrees Fahrenheit. Line a 12-cup muffin tin with the paper liners.

In a big mixing bowl, whisk flour, cornmeal, baking powder and cinnamon together.

In a separate bowl, beat egg, honey, milk, corn oil and sour cream. Stir wet mixture into cornmeal mixture until just combined.

Divide evenly batter between the muffin cups and bake for 18-20 minutes until a tester inserted in the center comes out clean.

30.Pumpkin polenta cornbread

This pumpkin cornbread is perfect for the Fall with some squash soup and salad. I love the colour created by the pumpkin puree.

Preparation Time-25 minutes

Servings - 9

Ingredients

- 16 ounces canned pumpkin puree

- 1 ounce softened butter
- 2 lightly beaten eggs
- 4 lightly beaten egg whites
- 4 ounces brown sugar
- 1/2 teaspoon baking soda
- 1 teaspoon salt
- 1 teaspoon ground cloves
- 1/3 ounce ground cinnamon
- 1 teaspoon ground nutmeg
- 8 ounces low-fat plain yogurt
- 16 ounces polenta cornmeal

Directions

Preheat oven to 350 degrees Fahrenheit. Coat an 8x8 baking dish with cooking spray.

Place pumpkin puree, butter, egg and whites in a food processor. Add the rest of the **Ingredients** except for yogurt and cornmeal to the food processor and process until smooth.

Transfer mixture to a large bowl and add yogurt and cornmeal. Mix until just combined and pour into baking dish.

Bake for 45 minutes until a tester comes out clean.

Conclusion

From sweet buttermilk cornbread to broccoli and cheese, there is a recipe in this cookbook that will suit whatever type of meal you prepare. When the occasion calls for a break from the traditional flour-based bread and you want something more filling, cornbread is the answer. The recipes are simple and take less than 30 minutes to prepare. After 15-30 minutes, you are on your way to enjoying a delicious loaf of freshly baked cornbread to satisfy your hunger.

Made in the USA
Monee, IL
20 February 2020